ABOUT THE AUTHOR:

Lungile Malumana was born on the 13th of December 1991 at Mapulaneng Hospital in Achornhoek. She is the sixth born of Alick Zala Malumane and the late Khombomuni Paulinah Ngobeni Malumane. She grew at up at Rolle Village in Bushbuckridge, Mpumalanga where she attended Soniye Primary School, Godide High School and matriculated in 2008 at Mugena high school.

She has Studied Business management, human resources management and occupational health and safety management. She started writing books in high school but her books were never published. "A love story of a troubled man "is her first novel to publish.

ACKNOWLEDGEMENTS:

I thank God for the wisdom, knowledge and understanding He has clothed me with. I thank Him for making this project to be a success.

My writing life would not have been possible without the support of many people whom I'd like to acknowledge and thank.

To my late mom KP Ngobeni Malumane, thank you for all the prayers you invested in me.

To my father Zala Alick Malumane thank you for being my rock. Your unconditional love and support keeps me going no matter what.

To my kids Karabo, Muhluri and Nkosihle Malumane I am grateful to have such amazing kids like you. The way you believe in me and my vision makes me feel blessed. I love you so much.

To my former English teachers Mr BB Ubisi and Mr Maluleke thank you for shaping me.

To my sisters Dineo Malumane and Phumy Ndubane, thank you for the support you keep throwing my way.

To my colleagues Moso Raeng and Bongani Harold thank you for believing in me and this project.

To my friend and colleague Abby Khosa Thank you for all the times you listened attentively to this book over and over again and still found it interesting. Thank you for all the inputs you've contributed. I am grateful.

To the readers I hope you enjoy this novel to the fullest.

Cheers!!!!!!

Growing up as a Pastor's kid I always knew I was expected to become one myself. My parents always told me it was my destiny and I cannot run away from it. They were grooming me to become a pastor as every pastor's kid is expected to. It is funny and sad at the same time how society expects every pastor's kid to take after their parents. I do not think society look at things at a different point of view. Pastor's kids are always expected to be like their parents. Any mistake a Pastor's kid make, the society always judge. It always comes down to "how can a Pastor's kid behave like this." One thing that they have forgotten is that whether it is a Pastor's kid or not, we are all humans. We are bound to make mistakes. We also have our own weaknesses and shortcomings just like any human being. There is nothing peculiar about being a Pastor's kid. We are human beings, not angels.

Well, my father was groomed by his own father to become a pastor. Grandfather was also a very well-known pastor of his times. It is something that has been running through the family blood line. It was said that great grandfather was also a Pastor, though his father was a traditional healer. Great grandfather was known as someone who came from a family of a very well-known and powerful traditional healer. That didn't stop him from becoming a pastor. Many respected him for following his own calling and not that of his father. It might happen that maybe his father gave him blessings to be able to become what he felt he was destined to be. Who knows?

My father was a very faithful man of God. In everything he did, he put God first. He lived his life for God. He loved God and the ministry with all his heart. He had a good reputation to a point where people were saying only good things about him. He was well respected and loved by many. Yes, he had enemies like any human being. In this life we are living in we are bound to have enemies whether we do good or bad. You can simply become an enemy to a person by lending a helping hand to another person. You can become an enemy by just living your life and serving your God ordained purpose. You can also become an enemy by speaking the truth, living by it and standing up for it. So, whether you do good or bad, you will always have enemies. Having enemies doesn't make you a bad person. You also do not have to speak bad or wish bad things to your enemies. Even the bible tell us to love our enemies and pray for those who persecute us. Us being their enemies doesn't mean they should become our enemies as well.

I always asked myself if I would ever be able to be like my father. I felt like his standard of living was way too high for me to ever be able to reach. I knew time would come for me to take over the family church as I was being groomed to become a pastor and a leader. The thought of it troubled my soul because I didn't think I was good enough to fit in my father's shoes. This man was way too perfect. He had all the qualities a good leader is supposed to have. He was a very humble and loveable man.

In our small, dusty village of Allendale everyone knew pastor Mabaso. That is how my father was addressed. He was a man of integrity, honesty, honour and a good heart. In all community development activities, he always made sure he avail himself. He would reach out and help whenever he could. Many regarded him as a good Samaritan. He strongly believed in feeding the poor, cloth them with clothes, love and comfort. Each and every month he would deliver food parcels to the needy out of his own pocket. Every year he provided stationary to the youth at church and nearby community development centres. He shared what he could with love and humbleness. All this made me doubt I could ever be like him when I took a closer look to myself.

I remember one of the days when my father went with me to attend a community meeting. At the beginning of the meeting my father was asked to bless it with prayer. "We humbly request our very own hero pastor Mabaso to pray for the proceedings," said the chairing lady. My father came forth, took the microphone and started praying for the meeting as requested by the chairing lady. He was indeed a hero in our community and everyone looked up to him.

People always said they were not surprised my father Pastor Rectify Mabaso turned out the way he was because he took after his father Bishop Reason Mabaso. It was said that grandfather Reason Mabaso was a very humble man. Even though he was tall, light skinned and very handsome just like my father, it is said he was a very principled man. He also served the community and in ministry with integrity. He preached the Gospel of Christ undiluted. He always stood up for what he believed in no matter what. He stood up for the truth at all times even if it meant standing alone. It is said that he was illiterate but he was very intelligent, smart and creative. All the qualities my father had were similar to grandfather's. Indeed it was a like father like son circumstance.

Grandfather, Bishop was the reason Mabaso married when he was thirty-three years of age and only had one son. Pastor Rectify Mabaso followed his father's footsteps and only married when he was approaching forty. He also had one son, me, Reliable Mabaso. Both my father and grandfather married one woman and each only had one child. Great grandfather had three children of which two were twins. Unfortunately, the twins passed away just after birth. He was then left with one son, Bishop Reason Mabaso. On the contrary great grandfather had five wives and many children. One of his wives who happens to be my great father passed away after giving birth to great grandfather. It is said that great grandfather then left the Hluvukani Village and his family behind to start his own life at Allendale village. That was where he became a Pastor and started his own ministry.

I always asked myself how these three Mabaso men managed to stay away from sin, served God in truth and in spirit. They also only married one woman even though they came from the roots of polygamy. Deep inside I wanted a polygamous marriage just like my great grandfather, Xihumana Vutlharhi. It was just a wish that I knew would never come true for as long as my father Pastor Rectify Mabaso was still alive. I knew he would never bless such marriage.

Judging by everything that was happening in our times, I just couldn't picture myself to be like father or grandfather. With all the temptations, social networks, peer pressure, beautiful girls and smart technology, it was never going to be easy for me. It felt like it was going to be mission impossible.

Bishop reason and Pastor Rectify Mabaso knew how to deal with temptations in their times. They remained focus on their purpose which was to serve God wholeheartedly. They dedicated their lives to Christ, had self-control and self-discipline. They made sure they do not conform to the standard of this world no matter what. As for me, I felt like I was a little different from them. notwithstanding the fact that people said I was humble just like my father, but I wasn't sure I had the same qualities as him. His level of self-discipline was too high that I felt it was impossible for me to reach. It was only time that would reveal the kind of a man I would become.

My eyes were quick to notice beautiful girls. My dream future wife was a beautiful one as well. Whenever beautiful girls passed me, my eyes would start drooling. My heart would beat so fast as if I was competing in marathons. The only thing that kept me from acting on my desires was the fact that I already had girlfriend. A beautiful one to be precise. Becoming a Pastor was not something I was passionate about. It was not something I wished for myself. I felt I was not good enough to take over my father and become a pastor. Even today I still marvel at God's mysterious ways. It is so strange how God choose those that doesn't feel worthy of His grace and use them for His perfect will.

When I turned fifteen years of age, my parents decided to have a meeting with me. It was a beautiful sunny Saturday, a day I will reminisce about for the rest of my life. I was still lazing around my room as it was not a school day when mother came looking for me. "Reliable, your father and I want to have a quick word with you," said mother with a very sweet yet humble voice. She patiently stood at the door waiting for me to come out. I quickly reach out for a T-shirt at the laundry bin behind my door, put it on while slipping my toes inside push ins and came out. I followed mother to the lounge where we found Pastor Mabaso eagerly waiting for us.

When we entered pastor Mabaso was going through some notes on his diary so he quickly put his diary down and shifted all his focus to us. Mother, pastor Londiwe Mabaso went on and sat right next to pastor Mabaso. They both looked at each other and smiled. They then looked at me at the same time and smiled again. I just smiled back without any understanding of what all the smiles were about.

One thing I loved about my parents was their love for each other and the unity they had. The way they looked at each other even a stranger would notice how deeply in love they were. Their faces would lighten up whenever they looked at each other. They would also smile at each other so beautifully while keeping a marvellous eye contact. They loved each other dearly.

"Boy how are you doing?" asked pastor Mabaso with a smile. "I am doing well father, all is well. "I also replied with a smile. "How is school," proceeded my father. His tone and gestures were very different from the other days when he would ask me about school. Pastor Mabaso always asked me about school but on this day, he just sounded so different. I just couldn't explain what was different about his gestures and facial expression, but it was very different.

"School is great father; I am glad I listened to your advice and took commercial subjects." This time I replied with a fake smile. The reason for the fake smile was the fact that I chose commercial subjects just to please my parents. I had always wanted to be a doctor but my parents were strongly against it. They said doctors often contradict with the word of God. With that being said, it was going to be difficult for me to serve as a doctor and a Pastor at the same time. Those were my parent's point of view.

Doctors believe in facts and science while pastors believe in God and his miracle working powers. Doctors may say "this sickness cannot be healed," while pastors say, "there is no sickness God cannot heal." Doctors may say "you are unable to have children" while Pastors say, "there is nothing too hard for the Lord." Doctors may say "once you reach menopause you can never have children" while pastors say, "it is God who made Sarah to conceive at her old age." It was going to be very difficult for me to serve the two at the same time.

My second passion was law. I wanted to study law of not medicine. My parents were still against it. I wanted to specialize in criminal law, but they still argued it would go against our beliefs as Christians. They made it clear that they didn't want me to represent criminals in court or lie just to get my clients out of messy circumstances. All this made me let go of my dreams to become a doctor or a lawyer for my parent's sake.

My parents wanted me to become an educator. Both of them were high school educators and they wanted the same career path for me. They told me they chose this career path because it never contradicted with their beliefs. So, at the age of fifteen doing my grade 10, I chose commercial subjects and decided I was going to study teaching after matric. I was going to become an educator just to please my parents. My decision to study teaching made them so happy to such an extent that they started calling me sir Mabaso. They were so proud of me; they even told me I was going to become a very prominent educator. Maybe I would, maybe not. Only God knew my destiny at that point and time.

"Boy, your mother and I have realised that you are becoming a very handsome young man. You are growing up and as your parents it is our responsibility to prepare you for the adulthood life." After Pastor Mabaso's statement we all looked down and silence filled the room as if a ghost had just passed by. It was evident that they were uncomfortable with the topic they were starting and it also made me uncomfortable to engage with them. It looked like they didn't know how to proceed with the topic they started.

As much as they made me feel uncomfortable, I felt having a decent conversation with them was long overdue. I had spent fifteen years of my life doing exactly everything my parents expected. to do. The funny part was that my father even taught me how to walk like a gentleman who loved God. It was too much for me to bear but I had to be what my parents expected me to be. Slowly and surely, I was getting exhausted of not being able to be what I wanted to be just because I was a Pastor's kid. It felt so unfair, but I had no choice.

The only time I felt free to be myself was when I was at school with my peers, back at home I had to be a well-behaved Pastor's kid. My parents even chose friends for me. I was only allowed to befriend youth from pastor Mabaso church. Not just members of the church, but those who were well behaved just like me. The friends I had were chosen according to their family backgrounds, roles they played at church and their characters. Pastor Mabaso always told me that it was wise to choose friends well because bad company always corrupt a good character.

I was only able to hang out with friends of my choice when my parents were not around. I did all I could to make them proud of me. I had to agree with everything they said whether it was what I wanted or not. I was a yes ma'am, yes sir boy. Judging from the outside you would think I was living an awesome life, but deep inside I was lonely, empty and troubled.

"Boy, when I met your mother for the very first time, I was 30 years of age. We were both educators at Mugena high school situated at Hluvukani Village." That was pastor Mabaso now breaking the silence. Before he could even go further, I started to have some clue of where the conversation was heading. It obviously about when I was expected to marry and who I was supposed to marry. I felt so helpless and exhausted at the same time. A part of me really wanted to stand-up and run straight to my room just to avoid this kind of a conversation. I so wished it was possible for me to do that, but it was unfortunate that I couldn't. A well-behaved, respectful pastor's kid like me wasn't supposed to behave in that shameful manner. So I had to sit still and listen to whatever they had to say to me.

"We developed a very good relationship as colleagues and eventually became friends. I never even thought of proposing her because I was still waiting for my father's approval with regards to relationships and marriage," said my father with a humble tone. His facial expression made me realise he felt exactly how I was feeling when he had to allow his father to run his life for him. I sensed a little bit of sadness although he was trying so hard to hide it.

"Your grandfather had to play his role as my father and pastor by choosing a woman that would be suitable to be my wife," he proceeded. "It was not only about marrying a woman suitable to be my wife but also a woman who would be able to play her role at church as a Pastor's wife. I had to understand that it was no longer only about me but the ministry as well. So I trusted my father to find a suitable helper for me." They both looked at each other with a smile as if what pastor Mabaso said was the best thing that could ever happen to them. They gave each other affectionate eye contact while smiling. I looked at with so many unanswered questions at the back of my mind that I knew it was impossible for me to ask.

“I was also waiting for my pastor to find a suitable partner for me, “said my mother. She said it with pride and confidence. “Our pastor always taught us about self-discipline from an early age. He played a vital role in my life and I am the woman that I am today because of him. How I wish pastors of today can be like Pastor Maluleke.”

Everything my parents said was a confirmation that they wanted to choose a wife for me. I could tell they couldn't wait to make that decision for me. “As handsome as I am what if a not so beautiful wife for me?” My spirit was so broken as all these questions were playing at the back of my mind. Nevertheless, I continued hiding my true emotions and kept smiling as if I understood everything they were saying.

“Honestly speaking I really thank God for people like Pastor Maluleke. If it wasn't for me him, I wouldn't have married such an amazing woman like you my love,” said pastor Mabaso as he gave my mom a sweet kiss on her forehead. Mother returned the lovely gesture with a sweet kiss on pastor Mabaso s chick. My parents were a perfect couple, perfect for each other. They had almost the same upbringing even though my mother was not a Pastor's daughter. This Pastor Maluleke indeed played a huge role in her life. She grew up without a father and she was from a very poor family. I could only imagine how difficult it was for her. She was fortunate that Pastor Maluleke played a role of a father and a Pastor in her life.

With all due respect, my mother was not really beautiful. She was dark in colour, tall and skinny. She had big eyes accompanied by a big forehead. If my father was not a pastor, I doubt he would have wanted to marry her. You know pastors says we are all beautiful in the eyes of the Lord. Even pastor Maluleke wouldn't have chosen her for my father of she wasn't humble, well-mannered and a Christian. Her good qualities are what qualified her for marriage, not beauty.

As for me, given any chance to choose for myself I would choose a beautiful, well-structured and curvy woman. Someone funny, outgoing, and a little bit naughty. My mother was a beautiful woman with a good heart, but she was just not the kind of woman I would want to marry. Pastor Mabaso and his wife were very boring. Sometimes I would listen to their conversations during their relaxation moments. Wow, everything was boring. They would talk about church, the bible, school, news and a little bit of sports. They were such a perfect match.

Because we were having an open discussion, I decided to man up and ask them some few questions. “Father, how did you ask mother to be your girlfriend and for how long did you date before marriage?” Pastor Mabaso looked at me in amazement . I believe he was amazed by how I asked the questions as I was not the type of person who would ask anything when they were talking to me. All I did was listen and agree. Maybe it was because they never really gave me any proper opportunity to ask questions when they were talking to me. Most conversations were about them telling me what to do, what to eat, what to wear, how to greet, how to walk and how to be a good child of God. There was no space for me to question anything.

"As Christians we do not date or regard one another as boyfriends and girlfriends. We do not conform to the standard of this world no matter what. When you feel time has come for you to marry you talk to your pastor, He helps you choose a suitable wife and talk to the woman on your behalf. if the woman agrees then you start to courtship. from court shipping then you engage after that you get married. We do not date like outsiders do," said pastor Mabaso with a very serious face.

My mother and I were quiet and listening attentively to everything pastor Mabaso was saying. "Bishop Mabaso, my father knew when I was ready to marry and start my own family," he continued. . He sat down with me and told me I was ready to marry and start my own family. He told me he already spoke with his pastor friend Mr. Maluleka to help him choose a suitable wife for me at his church. Pastor Maluleka then chose Londiwe, your mother to be my wife.

He gave my father the feedback that he got just a perfect match for me. A very humble, God fearing and educated woman who was also a teacher at Mugena high school. After that, they arranged a meeting for us." Pastor Mabaso sighed with relief, took a glass of water and drank. Then he continued with his love story.

He had mixed emotions when he was telling his story. At times he sounded sad, troubled, and lost in other times he sounded happy, relieved and peaceful. I couldn't tell exactly how he felt.

"Pastor Maluleke Came with Londiwe here at Allandale and we met at church with my father. When they arrived, we realized we knew each other from our workplace and we were so happy to see each other because we had a very good relationship at school. That was how I officially Met Your Mother as my future wife."

It felt like pastor Mabaso had forgotten about my equation of how long they got to know each other before they finally got married. I had to remind him so that I could get a straight answer. "Father, how long did you get to know each other better before you got married?" I asked with a very shy but humble voice.

"Eight years my son, I waited eight good years to finally make Londiwe Mrs Mabaso," he answered. His response gave me a shock of my life. I couldn't understand why they had to wait eight good years to get married. What is it that they were still trying to get to know for eight years?
"Father, but why that long?" I continued asking him so that I could get clarity. I really wanted to understand why they had to wait that long. for me six months would be enough. get to know each other and be certain we want to marry each other. If it was eight months or a year. I would understand but eight years.

"My son, sometimes things do not go according to our plans or wishes. if it was entirely up to us, we would have married within three months of our official meeting but we didn't have much choice," he replied with a sad voice.

“For The first three years after our meeting we were busy with our theology studies. Bishop Mabaso wanted us to graduate as pastors before we could get married and take over his church. he also wanted to make sure your mother was the right woman for me. Because we were already working so we had to enrol for distance learning so that we could study while working. Believe me son, it was the most challenging times of our lives.” It was now becoming difficult for pastor Mabaso to hide his true emotions. I could see sadness all over his face. I could tell that he did everything he did just to please his father, just like I was doing everything to please him. It was evident that he was hurt by his father's decision but he had to please him regardless of how he felt.

From that moment I realized pastor Mabaso knew how it felt not to have a say in your own life. he knew how it felt to have someone else take personal decisions on your behalf. he knew the feeling of not being able to be with the woman you love just because you have to fulfil your father's wishes. That was when I said to myself “maybe when time comes for me to marry, he will let me make my own decisions as he knows how painful it is for someone else to choose a wife for you and when to marry.” At least my father and I had something we could both relate to. I thought, it would work to my advantage.

When I looked at my mother’s eyes, I saw the same pain that was painted on my father’s face. That was when I realized that their decisions grandfather took for them heart and left a scar in their hearts. What I couldn’t understand was why they didn’t stand their ground. why did they agree to everything decided by grandfather while their hearts said the opposite? Why did they sacrifice so much just to make Bishop Mabaso happy? After a moment of silence pastor Mabaso tried to hide his pain by smiling at the both of us, he then proceeded with his story.

“Just After we graduated from Bible school, Bishop Mabaso ordained me as a pastor. He also gave me strict instructions that I was expected to lead the church for five years before marrying your mother. It was not easy but I had to understand that he was doing it for my good. He had to make sure I had the ability to lead the church without any distractions. he always told me that married life was very difficult and its difficulties has the potential to affect the ministry negatively so I had to be matured enough to be able to manage both. I was very fortunate because your mother was very patient with me throughout the entire process. as difficult as it was, she stood by me no matter what. that is what makes her a very special woman,” he said with a very beautiful and truthful smile.

“At the age of 38 I finally married your mother. two years into our marriage my mother passed away. A year later Bishop Mabaso also passed on. that is the story of our lives, son.”

We all found ourselves in a moment of silence. I was busy digesting everything they had just told me. the difficulties they faced along the way, how they overcame together and finally got married. My mind was full of questions and it became very clear that most of them will be left unanswered for the rest of my life.

"When do you think I will be ready for marriage?" I asked both of them while keeping eye contact because I wanted to witness their facial expressions towards my question. I really wanted to know what their expectations regarding my life was, as everything I did was for them.

"I Would prefer that you marry earlier so that you can give us many grandchildren. Marrying late delays, the process my son. Look at us, we had you at the age where we were supposed to be looking after our grandchildren. That is not the life I wish for you." My mother's response gave me comfort that they do not want me to travel the same journey they did in order to please grandfather. They had to please him at the expense of their own happiness. I also didn't think I was strong enough to go through such experience, I just couldn't.

"Do you by any chance have a girlfriend?" Asked my mother. Her question took me by surprise to a point where I really didn't know how to respond to it. I was caught up between telling an honest truth or a lie. I wasn't sure if they were going to accept my truth.

The truth was that I did have a girlfriend that I had just met. We were both doing gradec10 but she was doing maths with physics while I was doing commercial subjects. She was a very beautiful young woman, very beautiful. She Had big eyes, small lips, long black hair and she was short in height. She was my first love and we were so deeply in love with each other. I loved the fact that I was also her first love. I thought to myself "maybe my mother was asking my question because she was ready to accept my truth."

"Yes, I do, her name is Joy. She is from the Mkansi family residing on the second street just before
Mahuvo High School." My parents face changed in a blink of an eye just by hearing that I had a girlfriend. I became a little bit confused because for a moment I thought I was telling what they wanted to hear. I should have known it was just a trap. I really didn't see it coming, not at all.

"At the age of fifteen your mind is already conformed to the standard of this world," asked my father with a very aggressive voice. "Calm Down my husband please do not forget that his is supposed to be an open discussion meeting," said my mother while holding pasta Mabaso's hand with an attempt to keep him calm. Pastor Mabaso looked so angry and disappointed in me at the same time. My mother on the other hand was unpredictable, I couldn't understand her true emotions at all.

"Son, I am glad that you answered my question truthfully. However, you must remember that we are different from others and we do things differently. As your parents we expect you to part ways with that girl and focus on your studies. Your father and I have already made important decisions on your behalf," she said while brushing pastor Mabaso's hand.

It felt like my waist nightmare was becoming a reality. People always gossiped behind my back that my parents would choose their wife for me just as Bishop Mabaso did for my father. Knowing all this didn't stop me from thinking that my parents would maybe change their pattern but I was wrong.

"You Will finish high school at the age of seventeen, she proceeded. "Then You will start with your degree in teaching and in four years' time you will graduate and become a professional teacher. By the time you graduate you will be twenty-one years of age. At the age of twenty-two you will be ordained as a junior pastor and you will get married at the age of twenty-three." She said all this with a bit of a smile in her face just to bribe my feelings.

I started to realise that they had my whole life planned on my behalf. I bet they already knew what I was supposed to do with my first salary, the type of a car I was supposed to buy, what type of ring to buy for my wife and when to have children. "It It's clear that my life will never be mine as I will have to live according to their wishes and plans," I said to myself with a heavy heart.

"Yes, very soon you will know of the perfect woman we have for you. Her parents are also grooming her to become a wonderful pastor's wife. She is from a very good family with principles and her father is also a pastor. Now all we need from you is to stop this nonsense of having a girlfriend. Cut ties with her and focus on your studies. if you feel bored, the church and all its programs will keep you busy. There is no need for you to have a girlfriend. This meeting is adjourned, you can leave. His closing statement was said with a very aggressive tone. I couldn't say anything further because the mood had totally changed.

I stood up without saying a word and went straight to my room. I was so disappointed at my parents for planning my entire life on my behalf. Mostly I was disappointed at myself for failing to stand my ground and tell them my dreams and goals. I never wanted to be a pastor, which was just not what I wanted for myself. I also never wanted to be a teacher, but what choice did I have? I had to fulfil my parents' wishes. I knew I would have to study teaching, become a pastor but I didn't know how I was going to stop my heart from loving joy. A heart wants what it wants no matter what the mind says.

As soon as I went back to my room, I reached for my cell phone and called Joy. M y heart and soul was longing for her. I knew talking to her would help ease the pain and confusion I was experiencing at that very moment. There was something in her voice that brought me so much comfort and happiness. She had a healing voice. As soon as you answered my call, I felt so much better and comforted that I forgot everything my parents said.

I knew that she was all I wanted. My heart was refusing to let go of her, I just couldn't. Whenever I spoke with her, I felt like everything was going to be okay. I felt like I was going to be fine. The connection we had was so strong and real. We spoke over the phone for almost an hour. Our conversation was all about our dreams and lives after matriculating. We had a very beautiful and meaningful conversation that I forgot I was told to end things with her.

Few days after the meeting I had with my parents, everything they said started to play at the back of my mind word by word. All that did not stop me from loving joy. That was when I realized that nothing had the power to stop me from loving the woman, I had chosen for myself. That was the one thing that made me so eager to go against my parents' wishes with regards to my love life.

Time passed by and my parents never asked if I had broken up with joy. I believed they assumed I did because I was a good son who always did everything I was told to do. They had faith in me that I would do according to their wishes. Unfortunately, this time around I couldn't. I couldn't betray my heart for their sake. My love for joy grew stronger each and every day that we became more closer day by day. We shared a lot of beautiful moments together.

A year passed by and our relationship grew stronger. As young as we were at that time, we knew we were meant for each other. I could tell that she was the rip of my ribs just as the Bible says. The way we connected said a lot about our love for each other. We both passed our grade 10 with flying colours. Being in love didn't cause any disruptions on our academics. We encouraged each other to study hard because we both believed in education. We both wanted a brighter future through education. Our goals aligned, our dreams connected and our Purpose became one.

My parents were very happy that I passes grade 10 with good marks. It reassured them that I was focusing on my studies just the way they wanted me to. Pastor Mabaso couldn't stop telling me how proud he was after he saw my School Report. "I am very proud of you son, very proud." He said with a boastful tone. The way he said how proud he was of me really pleased my heart. It was the best feeling ever. I do not dispute that I did not like how my parents were literally running my life but making them proud remained my priority. I didn't want them to be disappointed in me in any way. I had told myself that the only time I would have to disappoint them was when I marry the woman of my dreams. The rest, I was willing to do as they wished. I was ready to sacrifice everything except for my relationship with joy. That was not negotiable. Dating for a year made us realise that it was possible for us to have a future together. We realised that we wanted to spend the rest of our lives with each other.

With us being together for a year, Joy decided it was time to introduce me to her family. The Nkuna's were such a lovely family and their hearts were full of love. They accepted our relationship and welcomed me with warmth and joy. They took me as one of their own. When Joy first proposed I should meet her grandparents I was very sceptical because I was afraid of rejection. I thought they would probably think I was not good enough for their beautiful and intelligent granddaughter. Whenever she brought it up, I would change the subject because I didn't feel ready. She kept nagging until I gave in and agreed to meet her grandparents.

It was on the 14th of march and it was her birthday. She invited me to the birthday dinner she had planned with her family. It was perfect and suitable for both of us as it was on a Saturday. I fed my parents lies that I was invited to a birthday dinner of one of my friends. Had I told them it was joy's birthday celebration they would have made sure I do not set a foot to her place. They only allowed me to attend because they had the impression it was a male friend's celebration. Pastor Mabaso even helped me choose the best outfit for the celebration. Little did he know that he was preparing me to meet my future in-laws. I looked very neat, smart and handsome.

The set up of the dinner was at the Nkuna's backyard. It was kept cosy and simple. Everything was well organised and perfect. Joy really impressed me by the way she went all out to make sure everything looked perfect. She had set up a table with ten chairs, put some beautiful fresh flowers from her backyard and some few balloons pinned up against the wall. The table was covered in a white and gold tablecloth. The chair covers were also white and gold. It was nothing big but it was beautiful and special because it was well planned. Her grandparents were dressed in a very elegant and colourful Tsonga traditional attire. Grandma Sarah complemented her look by adding a traditional necklace that matched with her bangles. She looked like a Tsonga Queen. Her four siblings were also wearing white traditional dresses with colourful high heels.

As for my woman, she was more beautiful than the rest. She was wearing a gold, long but tight dress that was showing her lovely shape very well. Her curves were well accommodated by the dress. On top it also accommodated her cleavage so well. She put on black high heels with gold stripes. Her make-up was well done and the red lipstick made her look more attractive. She put on gold necklace, bangles and earrings. It was my first time to see her in such a beautiful state. She was beautiful everyday but on this particular day she looked like an angel. Her long black her was well combed and pushed back neatly. She added a back and gold hair clip that suited her perfectly. The way everyone was well dressed you'd swear it was our wedding day.

We had a lovely dinner and Joy introduced me to her family as her boyfriend. Her grandparents accepted me just like that without any interrogations, deep lectures or judgments. All they said was that we must take a very good care of each other as we travel the journey of life together. Their warm welcome made me love joy more. They reminded me that making Joy my girlfriend was the best decision I could ever make. This encouraged me to love her more and take a very good care of her. I made up my mind from that day that I was never going to disappoint them in any way. After the way they accepted me, I felt I owed them that much.

I was already trying my best to take care of Joy. From the monthly allowance I was receiving from my parents, I made sure she lacked nothing. I made sure she had enough cosmetics to last her for the month or so. Uniform and stationary, I made sure she had enough. I also made sure she had enough money for lunch at school each and every day. I provided her with everything she needed and showered her with love. Every chance I would get, I made sure I showed her how much she meant to me.

It was not easy to fit her into my weekend schedule as I was expected to be at church playing keyboard or guitar for the choir and worship team but I made it a point that every little chance I got I spent it with her. Spending time together, sharing our dreams grew our love strong and brought us closer than we could have ever imagined. She was not only my girlfriend but my best friend and mentor as well. She meant everything to me.

It Is true that when the heart decides there is nothing the mind can do. When the heart thinks, the mind becomes useless. Matters of the heart cannot be easily controlled. When a heart loves it loves for real, nothing else matters. Love has a way of making a person feel weak and strong at the same time. It has a way of making a person feel so alive and lifeless at the same time.

Love has a way of making a person happy and anxious at the same time. Love heals and kills at the same time; love can become a sickness and a cure at the same time. A moment of love feels like a moment of madness at the same time.

I experienced very confusing feelings in my relationship with joy. My love for her made me weak and strong at the same time. It gave me a reason to wake up each day and made me also afraid I'd wake up and find her gone. I loved her with all my heart and soul. At times I felt like I was losing my mind whenever I thought of her. She had this unexplainable effect on me. I never wanted to imagine my life without her. I never wanted a future that did not include her. All I wanted was a life story that she had to be part of until the end. I could feel it that only death could ever bring us asunder.

I believed she felt the same way too. She gave me the same love I gave her. Every chance she got she told me how much I meant to her. She made me feel like I was the only man on earth. She always told me that she believed we were meant for each other.

Joy and I were both virgins when we started our relationship. She made it crystal clear to me that if I loved her enough, I would wait until she turns twenty-one. I respected her decision but it was not something easy to live with. As for me I was only a virgin because my girlfriend wanted us so to wait. if it wasn't for that, I was ready for action. My love for her made me respect her decision.

Kisses and hugs were allowed here and there but the rest was a no-go area. She was too strict when it came to that.

One fateful night my classmate Thabo Dube invited me to his house party. It was his birthday so he decided to throw a house party for his friends and classmate. We were told to bring along our partners. Thabo was a son of our local councillor Mr. John Dube. His parents status made it possible for my parents to allow me to attend the party so I invited my girlfriend joy. I called her grandparents as well and ask for their permission to take joy with me to the party. I promised to bring her home safely. Her grandparents granted my request and urged me to take a very good care of their granddaughter. I promised to keep her safe for their sake. Joy was excited that I chose to take her with me to Thabo's party. Everyone in our peers was talking about the party some wished to attend but unfortunately without an invite it was impossible.

The day of the party finally arrived and everyone was supper excited. Pastor Mabaso even borrowed me his favourite white Mercedes Benz to use for the local councillor's son party. He also gave me a thousand rand to purchase anything I would need for the party. I used some of the money to arrange special transport for Joy. I arranged a metered taxi to fetch her from her home and drop her at Thabo's place. I couldn't risk fetching her with my father's car because people would start talking and it would jeopardize our relationship. The best I could do was pay for her transport.

I made sure I arrived at the earlier so that Joy could find me there. I didn't want her to feel uncomfortable or unwelcome in my absentia. Thabo's parents were away for the weekend so we had the whole house to ourselves. They were such cool parents. They gave their son space to celebrate his birthday with his friends without any interruptions. I wished Thabo's parents were mine. They were so open minded and selfless. My parents would never allow me to host such a party at home. Never.

Anyway, I had to accept and make peace with the kind of parents I had. I had to understand why they were overprotective and strict. I believe they had my best interest at heart because they loved me so much. Constantly complaining wouldn't change anything anyway. The best thing I could do for myself was to accept.

The dress code was black jeans and white T-shirts for guys and white mini dresses for the girls. I made sure my woman had the right outfit for the party because I did not want her to feel like she didn't belong.

Thabo had invited all beautiful girls from local and as far as Nelspruit. He used his father's influence in politics to invite sons and daughters of businessmen and politicians. All the local spoiled brats were also part of the party. I believe I was invited because my father was well known, a little bit rich and I was his classmate as well. As for joy, it was only because she was my partner otherwise, she wouldn't have been invited or welcomed.

Most of the guests were dropped off at the party by their rich parents and some were borrowed cars to use for that day. Everyone made sure they wore branded clothes. Most of the T-shirts worn by the guys were Fabiano brand. Girls were wearing white sneakers such as Adidas. Bathu drip and Nike. My Joy was wearing a white, red bat short dress and Bathu sneakers. The dress revealed her curvy body so well. She was so beautiful and attractive.

On the menu was meat, pap and chakalaka. There was beef, chicken, pork, wors and impala meat. You just chose what you wanted to eat. If you wanted to mix all types of meat, it was also up to you. Juice and soft drinks were not served at the party except for alcohol. The only soft drink I saw were the tonic water bottles they used to dash strong drinks such as Gordon's.

There were different kind of snacks like biltong, dried fruits and peanuts. It was a birthday that had everything except for a cake. There was a catering company with its employees that made sure everyone had anything they needed from food to drinks. There was also a special deejay that was playing good music that everyone enjoyed. On the dance floor we saw various kinds of dance from slow jam to amapiano dance. Everyone was having the best time of their lives.

Joy and I had never tasted alcohol since we were born. We didn't know how it felt like to ne tipsy or plainly drunk. When everyone was busy with their drinks we also tagged along. We drank wine and amarula. The rest of the drinks we didn't bother trying them. The waiters kept the glasses of wine coming that we even forgot ourselves. I drank so much to an extent where I even forgot I was a Pastor's kid.

We were all annoying ourselves until Thabo started making moves on one of his guest by the name of Lelo. Lelo was a daughter of a well-known politician from Nelspruit. Everyone knew who she was. Her mother was also a well knows businesswoman who had lodges around Mpumalanga and Limpopo. Thabo had always wanted to make her his girlfriend but did not have the guts to do so. It was until he was drunk that he decided to make his move.

He danced right next to Lelo while whispering in her ears. One thing led to another and before we know it, they started kissing. Thabo's girlfriend Mary was in the bathroom when Thabo started circus. When she came back to the party, she was met by her boyfriend kissing Lelo. She didn't ask any questions or give anyone any chance to explain anything. She went straight to them and started hitting Lelo with few claps and fists. Luckily, we managed to stop the fight before it went ugly.

Lelo was bleeding on the nose and crying like a little girl. She kept screaming "I want daddy." Her personal driver rushed to the scene and attended to her. The moment he realised she was bleeding he rushed to the car a brought a small first aid bag with him. He cleaned her blood and took her with to the car. Thabo tried his level best to apologize on behalf of his girlfriend but the damage was already done. As for Mary, she never bothered with any apologies. She kept saying "you deserved it and more." Meaning had we not intervened in time, daddy's little girl's would have been rearranged. The funny part is that the incident didn't stop the party. As soon as Lelo and her driver left, the party continued.

Joy and I had the best time of our lives. I believe everyone enjoyed the party as much as we did. Even today I do not remember some of the things transpired that night. I do not remember when the guest started leaving or what time the party was officially declared over. I do not remember what time the music stopped playing or what time the catering company left. All I remember is how I woke up at 3am in Thabo's room with Joy. Both of us were naked. We didn't remember anything at all. As soon as we woke up, I drove Joy to her grandparents place and quickly rushed home. When I arrived home, I parked pastor Mabaso's car and rushed straight my room to sleep.

I overslept that I didn't even hear my parents preparing for church. I didn't even hear what time they left. I was so glad that they didn't bother waking me up to go to church with them. At least I was not the only person playing instruments at church. Pastor Mabaso had trained most of the youth at church on playing all the instruments we had. My absence wasn't going to affect the church service in any way.

Back at school Thabo's party was the talk of the day. From how everyone was dressed up, the food, drinks and the fight between Lelo and Thabo's girlfriend. Everyone couldn't stop talking about the presence of all the beautiful girls that also happened to be daughters of politicians and businessmen. Thabo became more famous at school, on the community and he was also trending on social media. I was lucky that my parents were not fans of social media platforms, otherwise I would have been in big trouble. There were videos of us having gun that was trending. The kind of fun we were having was not what my parents would be proud of. They would surely be angry and disappointed in me.

Jo and I sat down and tried to remember what transpired on the night of the party but our minds were blank. We didn't have any single clue of what happened, what we did, how we ended up in one bed but one thing for sure was that something happened. We were very reckless and wee regretted it but it was too late for that. We had to accept it and work on forgiving ourselves for the recklessness. We decided to get over it and pretend the party never happened.

Life went on and we continued with our relationship. I continued to live a double life of pretending to be a good son at home and Joy's boyfriend at school. I became so good at it that my parents never suspected a thing. What surprised me was the fact that they didn't give me a hard time with regards to Thabo's party. They never bothered asking why I came back home at around 3am. The only thing they asked was how the party went and whether I enjoyed myself. That was it.

Two months after the party Joy called and ask to talk to me face to face. It was a Thursday evening and I was very surprised that she wanted us to meet during late hours. I asked her what it is she wanted to discuss that couldn't wait until the following day at school. She said it was urgent and couldn't be discussed over the phone. She urged me to go and see her at her grandparents place. As soon as she hung up, I quickly asked for my parent's permission to go out and meet Thabo. I told them I urgently needed some previous question papers that would help me with a school assignment that I was busy with. The granted me permission and offered to borrow me mother's car for conveniency purposes. Unfortunately, I couldn't take the car because I was going to Joy's place and we had to be discreet.

I walked to Joy's place with so many questions at the back of my mind. I couldn't stop wondering what was it that Joy urgently wanted to discuss with me. Something too important to be discussed over the phone. I even thought maybe she wanted to end our relationship. I kept thinking and wondering if I had done anything wrong. I couldn't remember wronging her in any way. "Maybe she doesn't love me anymore, or maybe she met someone better than me?" I kept asking myself too many questions without any answers. I tried to figure out what could be the problem but I failed. I had to try and calm myself down otherwise I would lose my mind.

When I arrived Grandma Sarah welcomed me and told me Joy had locked herself in her room the whole day. I was told she refused to eat anything and couldn't stop crying. I knocked at room and she quickly opened the door the moment she heard my voice. Her eyes were red and swollen at the same time. It was evident that she had really been crying for some time. Before I asked her anything, I held her closer to me and gave her a long hug. I told her everything was going to be okay.

After managing to comfort her, we sat down on her bed right next to each other. She looked at me and tears started rolling down her again. I started to realise that whatever it is had to be very serious for her to be in such a state. She stood up, reached for her schoolbag and took out a pregnancy test. It was obvious she had already done the test. So, before she said anything I realised she wanted to tell me that she was pregnant.

I looked at her, wiped tears off her face and kissed her forehead. I told her once more that everything was going to be okay. I didn't know how it was going to be okay but I had to keep her calm. We sat down again and this time round she was no longer crying. I believe she was ready to have a conversation with me.

"Babe, I am pregnant. I missed my periods twice and I decided to buy pregnancy tests. I brought two of them and the results are the same." For a moment I got lost in deep thoughts. I didn't know how to react to the news. I was scared, confused and disappointed at the same time. I just didn't want to show her my frustrations at that moment. I gave myself enough time to think before I could respond. It was a very sensitive issue and I needed to tread carefully. She was already emotional; I didn't want to make her worse.

"How do you feel about it?" I asked her politely. She looked at me and nodded. "Babe I am so sorry for being reckless at Thabo's party. I believe these are the consequences of that night. It was never my intention to shatter you in this way. I understand you are hurt and confused, but I need us to discuss how you want us to handle this whole thing," I kept quiet for few seconds waiting for her response. She kept quiet still. She let go of my hand and distanced herself from me. I stood up and followed her. I held her hand and politely asked that we talk about it.

"I am not ready for this child," she said with a heartbroken voice. "This was never a part of our plans. I just cannot have this child. I want an abortion." She couldn't look me straight in the eyes after her response. I was angry and sad at the same time. Her response made me think she didn't love me enough to carry my child. Maybe she didn't want anything that would bind us forever. Yes, I was not ready to have child. It was something we never planned but the thought of abortion gave me goosebumps. It gave me skin rash. I did not want her to abort my child.

I immediately let go of her hand and stormed out of her room. I was failing to control the anger that was burning inside of me and I didn't want to say bad things to her. My only solution at that moment was to walk away from her. She followed me up to the gate while crying and screaming on me. She started behaving like a crazy woman that Grandma Sarah had to intervene. She politely asked us to go back inside the house and have a decent conversation. We both calmed ourselves down and went back inside the house. We followed her back to Joy's room where all three of us sat down.

"What is the problem? Why are you both behaving like hooligans," asked grandma Sarah. What I liked about her was the fact that she was a straight talker who didn't like beating around the bushes. She was courageous enough to call a spade a spade no matter the circumstances. We had to think hard before responding to her questions so that we do not find ourselves in the firing line.

"Grandma please forgive me for what I am about to tell you. I know you will be hurt and disappointed at the same time. Please find it in your heart to forgive me." Joy responded to Grandma Sarah while sobbing. Of all the plans joy and I had, pregnancy at this stage was never part of it. Joy had told me that she wanted to make her grandparents proud by getting education first, get married and have kids after. She never wanted to have a child while in high school. I knew these news that we were about to tell Grandma Sarah was going to be a huge disappointment. She'd be so disappointed in us most specially because she supported our relationship and gave us her blessings. She trusted us to be responsible enough to focus on our studies but we failed her.

"Grandma, I am pregnant and I think it's been two months now." Grandma looked at Joy with a smile, wiped tears off her face and gave her a long hug. Her reaction really confused me because I thought she was going to scream and shout on us. I thought she was going to tell us of how we've disappointed, failed and broke her heart. Instead of lecturing, she was comforting joy. Though she was smiling and comforting joy, I could see a little bit of disappointment in her face. I believe she was hiding her true emotions so that Joy can calm down and feel comforted.

"My grandchildren, I knew Joy was pregnant but I was just waiting for her to realise that she was pregnant. I saw all the signs a week just after the party you both attended. I took my time to process everything and deal with my true emotions. The hurt, the disappointment and the anger I felt. I dealt with it all and made peace with it. When I realise, I never thought she would fall pregnant at this stage more specially because she had shared her dreams with me had dreams of becoming a doctor getting married and having a wonderful family.

"Joy, as painful as it was, I had to make Peace with the fact that you are pregnant and there is nothing I can do about it. Crying over spilled milk could not change the circumstances. you have both disappointed me and it feels like I have failed you as your elder. I expected way better than this. Am I still angry? No, I'm not. I believe if we all work together, they both of you can still have the future you desire."

Grandma Sarah spoke softly but her words cut so deep. We had failed her in a way that she never thought we would. The pain of listening to how have hurt and disappointed her was so unbearable.

I found myself weeping like a little girl who lost her favourite doll because I felt the pain we had infuriated in her life. The room was filled with anguish as all three of us ended up weeping. It was just too much for all of us.

After a moment of letting our feelings get the better of us, we finally calmed ourselves down. The crying session helped us a lot as we were all ready to have a decent conversation after it. It also made me feel like a burden had been lifted off my shoulders as I felt calmer and lighter than before. Joy was no longer crying as well and she looked calmer than earlier on. We had to be calm in order to discuss a way forward.

“Grandma Sarah, I hope you find it in your heart to forgive joy in life for this pain we have caused you,” I said with a sad voice. Starting a conversation after the sobbing session was very difficult but I knew we had to talk about the pregnancy. It was getting late so we had to discuss and find a solution or a way forward before I could head home.

“What brought the fight between myself and joy was the fact that joy wants an abortion. I know and understand it is her body and she has every right to do as she wish but it doesn't sit well with me. I do not want her to have an abortion. I am not saying I am ready but I am saying I will do everything in my power to take full responsibility of this child. Also, I am not saying what we did was right but all I can say is that a baby is a gift from God no matter the circumstances.” I could tell joy was against everything I was saying because she couldn’t stop nodding her head in disagreement.

“I am not ready to be a mother, what about my future? I cannot throw away my future just like that, never. Joy voiced out her frustrations but at least this time she was calmer. As much as I understood her concerns, I still did not think abortion was the best option for us. “I will not allow you to abort this child joy,” I disputed. Grandma Sara sat quietly and gave us enough time to argue amongst ourselves. She gave us enough time to voice out all our concerns and how we felt about the situation without any interruptions.

When she felt we have said enough then she intervened and commanded joy to keep the baby. She told her it was not negotiable and made it very clear that under her roof there shall be no abortion. As for me, she told me to man up and take full responsibility of my actions. Above everything else what brought me delight was the fact that she offered her full support. We closed our conversation by concluding that I had to tell my parents of which committed myself into doing and promised to give them feedback as soon as possible. I then rushed back home.

I tried to sleep that night without any luck because I could not stop thinking about the fact that joy was pregnant. I kept tossing and tossing the whole night. The funny part was the fact that I had mixed emotions with regards to the whole situation. A part of me was not happy that we had disappointed our parents but another part of me was super excited that I was going to be a father. I couldn’t believe that God entrusted me with fatherhood. I even convinced myself that we were going to have a baby boy. I imagined how I would teach him how to play guitar and I couldn’t wait to watch him play soccer and ride his bicycle.

What cut my happiness short was the thought of breaking the news to my parents. Where do I even begin because they commanded me to end my relationship with joy? They failed to accept joy as my girlfriend, how would they be able to accept her as the mother of my child? It was something that I didn’t see happening. I knew they would never accept her and the baby but still I had to tell them the truth. Whether they accept or not was completely up to them.

The only thing I was sure of was the fact that I was not going to turn my back on my flesh and blood with or without my parents support. I had already sacrificed a lot just to please my parents so I knew I was not going to sacrifice my flesh and blood for them. All I could do was to let them know of the situation and leave the rest to them. if they accept then good, if they do not accept then too bad for them. As for me I was going to be the best father for my child.

Weekend finally arrived and I decided to break the news to my parents. I knew I had to do it boldly and stand my ground when coming to my decision of supporting joy. It was better for me to break the news to both of them at the same time so that I do not have to repeat myself.

That Saturday morning, we had breakfast as usual and waited until we were all done eating. "Before we leave the table there is something important that I would like to share with you," I said to my parents. They were both already in motion of getting up so they had to sit and listen to what I had to say. "Is everything OK boy?" My mother's question was coming from a place of concern judging by her tone and facial expression I could tell she was worried.

"All is well mother but there is something very important that you need to know. Firstly, I would like to apologize for what I am about to tell you. I want you to know that I regret it and if it was possible, I would change the current circumstance. It is unfortunate and with great sadness that this situation is beyond my control, for that I am very sorry." We all went into a silent mode for a moment and my parents couldn't stop staring at me. I could see they were anxiously waiting for me to break the news.

"I know you have advised me to cut ties with joy and I should have done as you advised but I didn't. I continued my relationship with joy behind your backs and as we speak joy is pregnant with my child." Before I could go any further pastor Mabaso stood up and left the dining room. Mother tried to convince him otherwise to no avail. He left my mother and I on the dining room sitting quietly for a while hoping he would come back to the table. Instead, we just heard the sound of the garage door and immediately he went out with his car. That was when we realised, he was not coming back to the dining room.

"Now Listen to me very carefully," said my mother. "I am not asking or advising you but I am giving you an instruction. You are going to deny that pregnancy and stay away from that girl. We are not going to allow you to ruin our reputation just like that. She is just not suitable for you. Leave her while you still can. Today I want you to tell her that it is not your child and you want nothing to do with her. I am not going to repeat myself."

"With all due respect mother, I am not going to do such an evil thing to Joy. I know the child is mine and I will not deny my own flesh and blood. I respect you so much as my mother but you what you are asking of me is impossible. Is your reputation more important than your first grandchild? Your own flesh and blood?" For the first time in my life, it felt so good to be able to speak up and stand my ground.

I was patiently waiting for my mother's response but instead I received a hot slap across my face. While trying to come to terms with what was happening, she gave me another slap. She kept the slaps coming until I stood up and ran to my room. I locked myself up and tried to calm down as I was so hurt and angry at the same time but I knew I had to do everything in my power to contain my emotions. She followed me and started screaming just outside my room. She called me all sorts of names like ungrateful spoiled brat, disrespectful boy and a fool. I listened to everything she was saying but I didn't come out of my room because I couldn't risk being beaten by her again.

It was for the first time that my mother raised a hand on me ever since I was born maybe it was because I had always listened to everything, I was told I had never challenged my parents in any way that was why I had never received any hiding ever since I was born. I had always been a good son that they were very proud of.

I spent the whole morning in my bedroom playing TV game and eating the junk food that I had kept for myself. Before I knew it was already time for church practice so I prepared myself as fast as Could and left for church. Usually, Pastor Mabaso would come and check up on us at church while we are busy with our practice but on this particular day he never showed up. That was when I realized that I was in deep trouble. I didn't allow what was happening to interfere with the church practice so I made sure that we practiced as planned and did my level best. I also made sure that we finished practice in time so that I could rush and see the mother of my unborn child before I head back home.

As soon as we finished practicing, I went straight to Joyce place and spend some quality time with her. although everything was still awkward because she was trying to come to terms with the fact that she was going to be a mother, we enjoyed each other's company. In the midst of all the emotional roller coast we were going through we still managed to connect. It was so amazing how regardless of the situation we were faced with we still had love for each other. We still shared the same love that we had shared before.

After spending quality time together Grandma Sarah advised us to go to the clinic so that joy could start with the antenatal care. We promised her that's the first thing that we'll do on Monday morning and head to school together as soon as we finish. As we proceeded talking about the pregnancy, she asked me if I managed to break the news to my parents. A part of me wanted to be honest with her but I didn't want to break joy's heart so I told them my parents were busy and I would speak to them as soon as they were free.

I knew eventually I would have to be honest with them so that they would know where I was standing with my parents with regards to joy and the pregnancy but I was just not ready. I knew it would break Joy's heart and I knew it would hurt Grandma Sara as well. I couldn't risk losing the woman I love or her considering abortion because of my parents rejection. There was just too much at stake at that moment so I had to lie. The way grandma Sarah was looking at me while telling the lie made me feel so guilty. It was like she could see through me though I wasn't sure of it.

Lying to the two important women in my life was not easy and it made me feel like a bad person but I had to do it for their own peace of mind. I was trying to protect them.

When I arrived back home it was time for dinner. We usually had dinner at 8:00 PM every evening. I found my parents in the dining room having dinner but my food was not there so I went to the kitchen to dish up for myself only to find they did not leave anything for me. I did not bother asking them anything instead I prepared a salad and bread for myself. I also didn't join them in the dining room as I had my dinner in the kitchen and went straight to bed after that.

The following day it was a Sunday and I woke up early to prepare for church. When my parents woke up, I was already done with gardening. I greeted them but they gave me silent treatment. Mother prepared breakfast for herself and pastor Mabaso. They sat together in the dining room having breakfast as if I was non-existent. I decided to make my own breakfast and sat by myself in the kitchen while having it. The silent treatment did not sit well with me but I decided I was going to give them space to Process the shocking news I broke to them. I believed it had come as a shock and they were still trying to come to terms with everything. The best thing I could do was to give them enough space to process it all. I believed when they were ready to talk to me further with regards to the pregnancy they would.

Every Sunday my parents would borrow me a car to go to church with. I usually left early to connect sound and ensure everything was in order. Mother and father would then join the service later on. On this particular day when I finished bathing, I went to borrow their car but I was not responded to. I decided to take a walk to church. Ehen, I arrived I prepared for the service as usual and ensured the sound was well connected. My parents arrived later on and it was business as usual. After the service, they left me behind while I was busy disconnecting the sound. That did not bother me much because I was expecting it.

Instead of going back home after disconnecting the sound I decided to go out for lunch with my friends. It was pointless to head straight home after the service just to experience the silent treatment I was receiving. I knew there were high chances that mother wouldn't count me in on the Sunday lunch as well so it was ideal for me to go and have lunch with my friends. After spending time with my friends, I went to check up on joy before I could head home. I made it a point that I arrived home late when my parents were already in bed because it wasn't pleasant passing them without any conversation. The silent treatment they were giving me was very unpleasant to a point where I didn't know how long I was going to be able to keep up with it. I had never experienced that kind of treatment since I was born.

A week passed by and I was still receiving the silent treatment from my parents. Every Monday they used to give me pocket money to last for the whole week but this time things were different. They stopped giving me any allowances, buying me weekly data and borrowing me cars. As painful and frustrating the situation was, I still kept my mouth shut. I spent most of my time locked up in my room just to avoid running into them. My focus shifted from everything that was happening to joy and our unborn child. I took my last cents on my savings account and arranged metered taxi for Joy and me to attend her antenatal care at the clinic. Joy became my priority nothing else mattered.

Joy's grandmother made a follow up with regards to informing my parents about the pregnancy. This time I told her I had broken the news to my parents and they said they would revert back to me with regards to a way forward. I did not have the guts to tell her they wanted nothing to do with joy or our unborn child. Though delaying the truth wouldn't change anything, I still convinced myself it was the best way to protect joy and our unborn child. I did not want her to be stressed in any way.

A month passed by and Grandma Sara made a follow up again with regards to the way forward my parents had said they would come up with according to me. Still, I gave her excuses after excuses until she got fed up. One fateful day she decided it was time to take a step forward because joy was already three months pregnant and it was starting to show. She decided it was time her family came to formally inform my family about the pregnancy. Joy was told not to make me away that they were coming to see my family and she did as she was told.

I was still on the dreamland when my mother knocked at my bedroom door. I was so surprised and happy at the same time because I had thought it meant the season of silent treatment had finally come to an end. I was punished for the whole month so I thought everything was finally going back to normal. As soon as I opened the door she came in and closed the door again. she then told me joy and her family were in the sitting room. Looking at the time it was around 5:00 AM so I panicked thinking maybe something was wrong with joy or the baby. Mother explained to me that the Nkuna family had come to inform the Mabaso family about Joyce pregnancy.

"Listen to me very carefully, today is your chance to free yourself from all this madness. I want you to think carefully before making any decision because you have two choices on the table. The first choice is to deny the pregnancy in the presence of both families and cut off all ties with her. If you can do that, your father and I will forgive you and move on with our lives as if nothing happened. The second choice is that if you accept the pregnancy you will leave with your in-laws. You will be expected to pack all your belongings and move out of this house as we cut all ties with you and disown you as our son. You will see how you move forward with life and your new family. The choice is yours." She stood up and left the room before I could respond.

After thinking long and hard about their choices ahead I decided that I was going to deny the pregnancy. I realized accepting the pregnancy would do more harm than any good. Being homeless and moneyless at the same time was going to put a lot of strain on Joy's family, herself, our unborn child and our relationship. Denying the pregnancy on the other hand meant I could still enjoy all the benefits at home and continue my relationship with Joy secretly. Though it was going to be very painful for her but it was worth it. Every cent I would get from my parents it would help provide for Joy' every need and our child.

When I arrived at the sitting room I was met by joy, her grandparents, uncle and my parents. Just by taking one look at me joy smiled with joy. Little did she know that I was going to break her heart into pieces. Her grandparents smiled at me as well because they didn't know I was about to shatter their grand daughter's life. Had they known, I do not think they would have even bothered coming to my family.

After sitting down, I greeted everyone in a very humble manner. Pastor Mabaso immediately went straight to the point and asked if I knew joy and her family. I agreed to knowing them and explained she was my ex-girlfriend. I further explained we broke up a few months ago. My response painted a beautiful smile on my mother's face because she realized I took her advice of denying the pregnancy and cutting ties with Joy.

As for joy and her family, my response gave them a shock of their lives. It was so shocking that almost every day I went to visit joy at her place and yet I was saying we broke up a few months ago. Her family looked at me with so much pain and disappointment in their eyes that it cut me so deep but I had to contain my emotions. Joy on the other hand failed to control her emotions as she started crying out so loud with so much anguish. She cried like a woman who had just lost a loved one to death. It pained me to watch her cry like that knowing I was the cause of her pain but I had to stick to my plan.

Her family asked again to get clarity on what I had just said they specifically asked if I was denying being the father of the unborn child joy was caring. I made it very loud and clear that I was denying the unborn child. I further explained that our relationship did not get into a point where we were intimate. Joy's grandmother became so emotional and looked down while wiping off tears that were dropping off her eyes. She thanked my family for our time and asked her family to leave. They did not bother saying anything further, instead they stood up and left. Joy couldn't stop crying even as they were leaving.

My mother couldn't stop telling me how bright she was that I came back to my senses and took her advice. Pastor Mabaso on the other hand kept quiet, he never said anything at all. When I looked at his face, he was no longer angry at me instead he looked hurt. It was difficult for me to understand where he stood. Whether he was in support of what I just did or whether he was disappointed in me for not standing my ground remained hidden in his silence.

A month passed and I had not heard anything from joy. I went to her grandparents place numerous times but I was denied access or any kind of information with regards to Joyce whereabouts. I kept dialling her number million times every day but it took me straight to voicemail. At school I kept going to Hitler's over and over again hoping to find her but it was all in vain. It was like she had just disappeared into thin air.

What frustrated me most was the fact that all the people close to her refused to talk to me. I tried her grandmother, siblings and classmates yet I failed to find any information regarding joy. I became a miserable and troubled young man. I wished sobbed I could at least hear her voice just to know she was alive and well. I wished she would just call me and tell me everything was O. how I wished I knew where she was who she was with and how she was doing.

There was no light that passed by that I didn't dream of her. there was no day that passed by without longing for her. I missed everything about her from her smell to her beautiful smile. Whenever I thought of her it felt like I was failing to breathe properly each breath felt like the last one. I tried so hard to live without her as I convinced my mind to focus on my studies but my heart failed me. My heart refused to let go of joy and all the memories we shared together.

I longed for her touch, her laughter, her naughtiness and how each time we spoke she would tell how much she loved me. I missed our long conversations over the phone every night before we went to bed. Life without her was so unbearable three times I even felt like taking my own life. it felt so useless to go through life without her because it meant I wouldn't have the future we had planned together. Honestly speaking I didn't know what I was living for anymore because joy was a part of my life. She was everything I ever wanted in life and everything I ever dreamt of in a woman. she was the woman I wanted to spend the rest of my life with. I just didn't know how I was going to face life without her.

What broke my heart more was the fact that she was carrying my child when she left. It broke my heart that I didn't know whether my unborn was still alive or not. It was difficult for me to live with the fact that there were high chances that joy has had an abortion. this killed me inside they by day, slowly but surely, I was losing my mind. Waking up each day was difficult, facing each day without her was more difficult it felt like Mission Impossible but I kept going because I didn't have a choice.

I couldn't stop wondering how things would have been if I had made a different choice. I blamed myself for failing to stand by joy and give her the support that I had promised her. I had failed myself joy our unborn and had grandparents. I sacrificed everything I had with joy just for my mother. I turned my back enjoy when she needed me most just to please my parents. I had failed as a man and as a father to be. Yes, my parents were proud of me but at what cost?

Since it was month end, I decided to take the monthly allowance I was giving joy to her grandmother. it was obvious that she knew Joy's whereabouts and had a way of communicating with her. So, I knew she was the right person to give the allowance to as I knew she would make sure Joy receives it. I even bought all her cosmetics and all her favourite chocolates. Inside the Pack I inserted a note written "I never stopped loving you and never will, I hope both you and our child are well." This was the least I could do after the mess I had created.

I called Grandma Sarah and begged her to receive the parcel on Joy's behalf. It was not easy but the end but at the end she agreed to meet me and receive the parcel. When delivering the parcel, I tried to get information about Joy's whereabouts but Grandma Sarah gave me nothing. She was not keen to have any conversation with me at all. I understood and respected her wishes because

I was the one to blame for everything that was happening. So as soon as she received the parcel and made it clear she was not going to talk to me about Joy, I left.

Though I still didn't know where Joy was, at least I knew she was alive. I was also relieved that I had managed to provide for her just as I used to. What I still had questions about was the existence of our unborn child. No one was willing to talk to me so I had no one to confirm its existence. All I could do was hope for the best. I even prayed for God to keep Joy and our unborn safe and sound just for me. I didn't think I would be able to forgive myself if anything had to happen to any of them.

At home I continued to be the perfect son I was expected to be although deep inside I was a very troubled young man. I did everything that was expected of me at home and at church. Although I

was playing my part, my behaviour at home completely took a roller-coaster. I still did house chores as expected but I completely stopped having any meal with my parents. I resented them wholeheartedly for what I had to put joy through because of them. This resentment made it very difficult for me to sit on the same table, play happy family and share a meal with them. I made sire I had my meals either in the kitchen or my bedroom.

During my spare time I made sure I spent the whole day at church giving instruments lessons to the youth. I made it a point that I got home late, ate my food and went straight to bed. I minimized having any encounter with my parents and only engaged with them when it was necessary and unavoidable. The lesser I saw of them the better it was for me because I did not want to end up taking my frustrations on them.

At school I gave my all because I couldn't wait to pass matric and go to varsity. I couldn't wait to be free from the toxic environment I was living in so I had to work hard to guarantee my freedom. My marks improved in such a way that my teachers were very proud of me. I just could not allow what I was going through to interfere with my studies in any way.

Every month I delivered a parcel of cash groceries with a love letter at Joy's place. I trusted Grandma Sarah to ensure the love of my life received everything. Each time I went to deliver I kept hoping to receive any news about Joy but my hopes did not bear any fruits. That did not stop me from making the monthly deliveries because I did not want Joy to lack anything. At least once a month I was able to express my love for her on those love letters that I kept sending. Even though there was no response at all but I was glad I reminded her just how much I loved her. My love for her kept growing regardless of our circumstances. I continued living a miserable life with a troubled heart and soul hoping maybe Joy would come back to me some day. I had to hold onto my faith no matter what.

One fateful day my faith repaid me in a way I never ever imagined. It was month end and I went to deliver my monthly parcel at Joy's place. I had a lot to deliver because it was festive seasons so I borrowed one of my friend's bakkie to load everything. Just after offloading, Grandma Sarah invited me inside the house for a cup of coffee. It came as a surprise because I was not expecting something like that from her but it was a pleasant one. We sat down and had a normal conversation while drinking our coffee with some mouth-watering biscuits. I was patiently waiting for her to present the purpose of her invite because it was obvious, she had some news to share.

"You broke Joy's heart in a very terrible way and it nearly destroyed her. I do not understand why you had to put her such pain and heartache when she needed you most. Anyway, it is all in the past now. Joy has delivered a healthy baby boy at Mapulaneng Hospital. His name is Miracle Nkuna." The news grandma Sarah broke to me were the best and just what I needed to hear. I stood up, danced and clapped hands because I couldn't contain the joy I had inside of me. It felt like God gave me a second chance to make things right. It was a chance to rectify my mistakes.

I tried to get more information regarding my son and joy but Grandma Sara denied me the chance. I was hoping she would allow me to see them but she refused claiming that Joy was not ready to have any encounter with me. As painful as it was, I had to respect her decision. So, I asked Grandma Sarah to assist me in compiling a list of everything Joy and my son needed. From diapers, baby cloths, bath sets, toys, coat bed, Joy's toiletries and some clothes. As soon as we finished compiling the list, I rushed to Thulamahashe Mall and bought everything. I also withdrew R1500 from my mother's account so that Joy may add anything I might have left. After the shopping spree, I rushed back to Grandma Sarah's place and dropped everything including the cash. This time I wrote a very long love letter dedicated to joy, the mother of my son.

"I was a fool to turn my back on you when you needed me most. It was not only you who needed me most but my unborn child as well. I cannot begin to fathom what I have put you through and I know I cannot take it back. If only I could turn back the hands of time, I would do things differently. It is unfortunate that I cannot take back the hands of time but it doesn't mean I have to fold my hands and let things be. I am here, ready to fix my mistakes and take full responsibility of you and my son. I have been miserable without you Joy. Please forgive me for all my mistakes and find it in your heart to love me again. I never stopped loving you and never will. I am praying for enough strength to be able to patiently wait for the day I will hold you and my son in my arms. I know God answers prayers hence I will hold on to my faith. Please reach out and let me know if you need anything else. I love you so much and please tell my son that daddy will meet him soon. Take care."

Of all the letters I had written to joy the past months this letter was the longest. I wrote this particular letter expressing my true Emotions and withholding nothing at all. Every Word I wrote came from the core of my heart and I hoped joy would receive it with a pure heart as well. My intentions were for her to understand how I felt about her and the whole situation. She remained the woman I wanted to spend the rest of my life with. My heart longed for her to a point where I could not picture myself with another woman beside her. Joy was their rib of my ribs flesh of my flesh and the bone of my bones the only woman God had specially created for me.

Back at home mother did not even bother asking me about the withdrawal on her account because I was busy preparing for varsity life so I was allowed to use her account. Pastor Mabaso had transferred enough funds into mother's account for me to be able to purchase anything I needed as I await my matric results. Money was never an Issue at all.

My parents had applied on numerous universities on my behalf, so I was only waiting for my metric results. I had even received an acceptance letter from numerous universities but my parents preferred the university of Limpopo. Joy had only applied at University of Cape town and Cuba institution of medicine as she wanted to become a doctor. I didn't have any further information on whether she was accepted or not. I didn't even know if she continued with her studies after she disappeared on me. All I could do was remain positive and hope for the best.

I was so proud that before she disappeared, I had managed to assist him with any costs regarding her applications to the universities of her choice. It was her dream to study medicine abroad and I supported her because I knew she would become a great doctor because she was a wonderful person. Not disputing the fact that she was not a Christian, she was very loud and naughty but she was everything I wanted in a woman. She had a caring heart, very respectful and selfless. Her spirit of Ubuntu was one of the qualities that made me want to spend my entire life with her. Her exteachers at school loved her so much because she was a very bright student.

The day all matriculants were eagerly waiting for finally came and as I searched for my name on the newspaper, I found Joy's name as well. She had passed with seven distinctions and I passed with five of them. This was one of the happiest days of my life and I was very proud of joy. After everything I put her through, she still managed to focus on her studies. she was indeed a strong, unique and special young lady.

Few days after receiving our metric results, joy and our son returned back home. she decided to send me a text message and ask for us to meet. I did as she asked and I was blessed to meet our son for the very first time. I felt so much in love with him from the moment I laid my eyes on him. it was a very emotional moment for me, meeting my own flesh for the very first time. he was so tiny and cute at the same time., he had a cute face, innocent eyes and a sharp nose. he was very light skinned just like his father. Meeting my own heart in a form of a human being was the happiest moment of my life. I was filled with so much joy relief contentment and peace.

Seeing Joy after so many months of a disappearance filled my heart with so much joy as well. We rekindled our love and created beautiful memories with our lovely son. everything was finally falling into place just as we had planned. Me, Joy and our son formed a complete family.

Joy informed me that the Cuban institute had accepted her and she was living in few days. I made a commitment to provide for our son in absentia and gave him my blessings to go and study abroad. we made arrangements to hire a nanny to look after our boy while we both study in our respective universities.

Few days later joy left for Cuba and I also went to the university of Limpopo to study teaching in order to fulfil my parents' wishes regarding my career. I still continued to be part of the worship team and played keyboard whenever I came home for school holidays. My parents were happy that I was still on the right path. I was slowly becoming the man they were grooming me to be as I was doing everything that was expected of me, but my heart still belonged to joy.

Joy and I spoke every day no matter how busy our day would be. we video called once a day and spoke for an hour or more. That was how we were sustaining our long-distance relationship. she promised to come back for me and I also promised to wait for her. it was going to be the longest seven years of our lives while she studies abroad but we understood very well that love is patient kind and selfless. the long distance didn't separate us instead we grew stronger each and every day and we fell so much in love with each other.

Her scholarship covered two flights per year which meant you could only come home twice a year.
It was too much for us and we both agreed we wouldn't survive that so we made an arrangements that twice a year I would have to fly to Cuba. money was never a problem as my parents gave me more than enough. I also did gigs on my free time and charged to play keyboard for events even at the campus so I always had enough to cover my costs to fly to Cuba. We agreed she would come home during Easter; festive seasons and I would visit her on June and September holidays. My parents never suspected anything because they didn't even know I had a passport and I made sure I was always on her good books.

My first trip to Cuba was on the 30th of March 2010. It is the day I can never forget as it was my first time to fly, first time to go abroad, and first visit to the love of my life. I had mixed emotions as I travelled to meet my one and only. My mind was all over as I couldn't stop thinking about my parents and how they would react if they were to find out that I went abroad. If they were to find out I was still in a relationship with joy they would be upset, heartbroken, and very disappointed in me. All these thoughts troubled my soul but it was a risk that I was willing to take in order to be with the love of my life.

"Father For Easter we have decided to go to Men's camp with my friends." Those were the lies I had to feed my parents in order for me to go and be with joy, the queen of my heart. "So this Easter we won't be with you at church?" asked my father. "Yes father, and for two weeks you will not be able to reach me on the phone as we have decided we will have to switch off our cell phones in order to concentrate on the camp. This camp is meant for us to shy away from the things of this world and have an encounter with God without any hindrance,' I replied to my father. It was a little bit easy for me to tell this lie over the phone because face to face I knew my parents would see through me. They knew me well enough to see if I was being truthful or deceitful. That was the reason why I had to use a phone to deliver the news because I couldn't risk being caught out. The last thing I needed was to disappoint my parents or the woman of my dreams because if they were to find out about my plans, I knew they would do everything in their powers to make sure I

do not go abroad and they would surely separate me from Joy.

The fact that my parents would never accept joy was of my knowledge. They failed to accept my unborn child, my own flesh and blood how would they be able to accept a total stranger? At this point they are acceptance towards joy was no longer any of my concern because my heart wanted to joy and that is it. when a heart wants what it wants you can never control it or advise it otherwise.

Well, my son I am so proud of you," said my father while we were continuing with our conversation over the phone. "I am certain your mother will be very proud of you too as it is every parent's wish to see their son become a responsible man. You have made me the happiest father alive," he said with so much pride and happiness. His response broke me deep inside, the truth about this matter hurt me to the core because I knew very well, I was telling him what his heart needed to hear but it was all a very big lie. "Do You need any financial help my son?" He continued while I was still trying to find the right response to his statement. "Yes father, any amount will be helpful."

The honest truth was that I didn't want any specific amount because I had already saved enough to cover for my trip and also spoil my woman. I didn't want to turn down his help hence I decided to accept any amount he was going to offer me. "It is not a problem at all, as soon as you hang up, I will transfer ten thousand into your account so that you do not struggle with anything. We love you so much and we are very proud of you son, May God be with you," concluded Pastor Mabaso. "I am So blessed to have you as my father and I want you to know that I do not take it for granted. I hope someday we will be able to sit together man to man and share the stories of our lives. I hope on that day you will understand why I had to make all the decisions I am making today and how much bravery it took for me to be able to take such decisions. I love you both, please pass my warm greetings to mother." I quickly hung up the phone because the guilt was getting the best out of me.

A part of me questioned the choices I was making but another part of me was happy and relieved. Throughout the trip the conversation I had with my father was playing at the back of my mind. I couldn't believe I had become the person that I was at that moment, a liar and a deceiver. "How Did we get here?" I asked myself so many times. My mind was asking all these questions but my heart was saying something else.

It is true what they say, when a heart speaks no one is able to speak against it. Once a Heart decides, the mind cannot fight back. I started to understand why people would say love can make you do silly things, take risks and become a person you never thought you would ever become in your life. My whole life I had been a very good son who did everything my parents expected me to do. they trusted me with their lives to a point where they would always send me to the bank whenever I was home entrusted me with a large sum of money. Mother would always deposit money into my account and ask me to make payments to certain people and settle certain accounts on her behalf. I was their golden son regardless of the drama with joy's pregnancy. Maybe it was because I took my mother's advice at that time and denied the pregnancy.

You see love can completely blind the mind. With love a person becomes a different person. Whenever I thought of joy I would think with my heart and not with my mind. Because they say love breaks and love heals, I didn't know if this love would break or heal me. if it would destroy or build. All I did was to follow my heart and where it was leading me and at that moment my heart was leading me straight into Joy's arms. I took all risks because of love.

When I arrived at Cuba joy was waiting for me at the airport and we took a local cab into her place of residence. She looked more beautiful in a well-designed red mini dress with black high heels. She wore a beautiful jewellery that complimented her dress. Just by one look at her I knew all the risk I took were worth it. she was the most beautiful woman my eyes had ever seen and my love for him made him more beautiful in my eyes. when she put her arms around me giving me a warm welcome hug my heart started beating faster than ever. It felt like I had just worn a jackpot. My body was so hot as if I had been put inside a burning stove. I started sweating instantly and my lips was unable to say out any word. Till this day I am unable to explain the feeling that I felt on that particular day. I believe she felt the same way too because I had to wipe plenty of tears off her face. I believe they were tears of joy because I had no doubt that joy loved me the very same way that I loved her.

When we arrived at her place of residence, she quickly prepared a hot bath for me so that my mind and body can relax. She put bath salts that smelled so nice and a lavender foam bath. she told me to take my time and relax inside the hot bath so that my body could feel fresh. I tried to do as she said but all my heart wanted was to hold her in my arms. 5 minutes was enough for me, I got out of the bathroom as fast as I could. Who would want to spend hours bathing while the purpose of the trip was to be with the queen of his heart?

The two weeks I spent with joy were so special as each day we made sure we enjoyed each other's company with love. on the last day of my visit she sat me down and said to me "love, if your parents choose a wife for you will you respect their wishes or go against them?" What I loved about her approach was the fact that she asked me in a humble manner. She didn't sound like the naughty, loud joy that I knew from high school. I understood though why she was asking me in a humble and well reserved manner because it was a very sensitive topic. It was a little bit difficult for me as I was not expecting her to ask me This kind of location in a moment where we were supposed to be saying our goodbyes in a proper manner.

"I know all your life you have been a good son and have always done everything that was expected of you," she continued with the topic. "How can I forget how you broke my heart into pieces when you chose your parents over me while I needed your support the most? Please do not get me wrong, I have forgiven you and I am past everything that has happened between us but I just need to know where I stand with you. Will you go against your parents' wishes and marry the woman you love or will you obey them?" I quickly rushed to the cupboard and reached out for a glass to quickly fill it with drinking water. the conversation was becoming too much for me and for a moment I felt like I was not breathing properly. I had two glasses of water and did everything I could to calm myself down. While calming down I was also having a very deep conversation with myself. "Will I stand up for our love, am I brave enough to go against the wishes of my parents, how do I defy my parents and choose love, if not how do I forget about joy, our son and honour the wishes of my parents?" I felt I was caught up between a stone and a hard place hence I had to think carefully before I answer the kind of question joy was asking me.

"Joy, I need you to trust me and the love we have for each other," I replied with a trembling voice.

"I have disappointed you before and believe me I was very miserable. I am not planning on turning my back on you and our son. I want you to know that no matter what happens along the way, love will always win. There is something going on our love shall conquer every obstacle we will encounter."

Honestly, it felt so unfair to me how I was expected to choose between my parents and the woman I loved together with my son. no man, no son deserves to be put in that kind of a situation. I wished I knew what to do when such day finally comes because it would definitely come. For me not to lose my mind I told myself that I would have to cross the bridge when I get there.

Although I had told myself I would cross the bridge when I get there by the equation gave me so much to think about. "Maybe if I could try to have a decent conversation with pastor Mabaso man to man he would understand my position." I say it to myself while thinking about my future with joy and our son. After our deep conversation, we said our goodbyes properly and took a cab to the airport.

From Cuba to South Africa all I could think of was the love of my life, Joy. it was impossible for me to forget the day she took me out to the movies during my visit. It was a first time we went to the cinema together. Personally it was at first time for me to go to the cinemas and it had never crossed my mind before that I would ever go to the cinema. Maybe I was too traditional, or maybe growing up I was just never exposed to such things. One's bringing plays a certain role in every person's life whether good or bad. It somehow impacts a person's future whether negatively or positively.

....

Life moved forward as we both continued focusing on our studies. Every weekend I travelled home because university of Limpopo was not too far from home. I continue to be the perfect son my parents desired me to be as I continued playing my role at church. what motivated me to go home every weekend was my son, miracle. Every time I went home, I made sure I went to see him and spend quality time with him. We would also capture videos and send it to joy via WhatsApp. I made sure I was a present father and fulfilled all my fatherly duties to miracle. My wish was for him to see and feel just how much I loved him as my son.

Four years later I was done with my bachelor's degree in education and ready to graduate. I couldn't believe I was finally done with my studies and ready to kick start my career. my parents we're very proud of me that they even planned a graduation party on my behalf. the event was planned to take place at church where different churches were invited to come and celebrate the milestone of pastor Mabaso's son. Local businessmen, community forum members and community at large was invited as well. pastor mother saw even invited local artists and wellrespected public figures to be part of the event.

Joy and knife got that because it was going to be a very important day of my life, she had to be part of it. We made her travelling arrangements in time so that she would be able to celebrate the special occasion with us. She still had to go back to Cuba after their celebration because she was not done with her seven-year degree. She was in her fourth year and still had three more years to go. The one thing that made me happy was the fact that we were managing our long-distance relationship just fine. Distance couldn't destroy the special bond we had because our love for each other was way too stronger than that.

The fact that their whole four years my parents never bothered to ask me about joy and my son troubled me each and every day. The fact that they moved on with their lives as if they never came to know about joy's pregnancy hurt me to the core. they never bothered to find out whether joy terminated or kept the pregnancy. Whether they heard their grandchild or not or how he or she was doing never bothered them at all. the only thing they cared about was their reputation. as much as they showed me love, I felt like they had some cruelty inside their hearts. Although this bothered me, I decided not to force them to love my son because for as long as I live, I was going to love and care for him.

After the graduation ceremony that was at the university of Limpopo I went home with my parents and the friends that were part of it. At home we had to finish off the preparations of the graduation celebration that was supposed to take place on a Sunday at our church. Two fat cows were slaughtered specially for the event as many people were expected to attend and the catering company was also hired for the special occasion. this was to ensure that all guests were served with food without any complaints.

On the day of the event, people came in large numbers to witness and celebrate with us. the venue was well decorated as if it was a wedding of a rich somebody. my parents spent a lot of money to make sure their event was blissful and they talk of town. it was a pity that they were able to spend a lot of money just to look good in the public's eyes but couldn't spend a single cent on their own grandson.

Joy arrived with our son and was ushered into the front row very close to my family. The ushers were just doing their jobs of ensuring all guests were well seated as they didn't know that Joy was the mother of my first-born son. As soon as Miracle saw me, he ran from his mother and came to sit with me where I was seated with my parents. He was four-year-old who didn't know that his grandparents never wanted or accepted him. He didn't even know who they were as they never bothered about his existence. As for me, he knew exactly who I was because I was a present father for the past four years and he was very fond of me.

Miracle was a copy of myself. Just by one look at him any person could see that he was my son. people who were gathered for the celebration started raising eyebrow, amazed by miracles presence as they were not aware that I had a son. As soon as my parents laid their eyes on Miracle, they realized that he was my son. I believe they realized it was the son I had denied four years back. The son they never bothered to ask about his existence. The son they refused to accept and love for the past four years. I wish I knew what was going through their minds When they laid their eyes on miracle.

Pastor Mabaso looked so emotional, but he was trying so hard to contain his emotions. He even greeted Miracle and played with him during the proceedings of the event. It's for my mother she ignored Miracle and put her full focus on the event. When it was time for them to have a word as written in the program, the program director called them forth. Pastor Mabaso was the first person to deliver his speech. He thanked everyone who worked hard to ensure the success of the event, praised God for such a beautiful event and thanked his wife for being amazing throughout the preparation process. He further stated how bright he was that I managed to finish my degree in record time. For all the efforts and hard work I invested on my studies, pastor Mabaso decided to bless me with a brand-new car. Everyone was singing, dancing and ululating when the car keys were presented to me. Joy quickly took Miracle from me so that I'd be able to go forth and accept my gift from pastor Mabaso.

When he was done with his speech, mother took over and continued telling everyone how proud she was of my achievement. She closed her speech by announcing our son getting married to a very humble young lady by the name of Jane. The crowd welcomed the news with pure hearts and celebrated with us. I quickly moved my eyes and fixed them right it's joy in our son's miracle. I saw just how broken joy was by the announcement mother had just made. She quickly took out a tissue in her bag and wiped off her tears.

This announcement broke my heart just as it broke Joy's s heart. It triggered memories that I had worked so hard to forget about. it felt like I had just gone back to the day I denied joy in our unborn in front of our families. I could feel that I was failing her and our son yet again. So I had to think fast and take a decision that I was going to live with for the rest of my life. The question was do I let go of joy and please my parents or do I stand up for our love? Is living a life like a troubled man worth it or do I choose love above everything else? I questioned myself as I was preparing to see my vote of thanks. After wrestling with my heart for around fifteen minutes I finally took the microphone from my mother and positioned myself to deliver my speech.

"I thank God for the gift of life, the wisdom and knowledge he has bestowed in me as well as his grace. I am grateful that God gave me such wonderful parents and I do not take it for granted. To Mr. and Mrs. Mabaso, thank you for everything you have done for me. You have been wonderful parents in my life and I feel honoured to be called your son." I took a few seconds break and drank some water. The venue was filled with silence as they were all paying attention to my speech. "All my life I have always this diet to please you as my parents. I focused so much on pleasing you that I forgot to please myself. I have done everything expected of me at home and here at church and I am glad that today I have finally made you the happiest parents by finishing my degree. However, I feel time has come for me to live my life as I see fit. I cannot continue living a lie that is slowly killing me deep inside and I hope someday if not today you will find it in your hearts to forgive me." Mother came closer to me and whispered in my ear "what do you think you are doing?" She knew where the speech was heading so she was trying to change my mind. unfortunately it was way too late. while she was trying to interrupt me, pastor Mabaso held her hand and laid her back to their seats so that I may proceed with my speech.

"Five years back I turned my back on the woman I love and our unborn son," I continued. "I denied my own flesh and blood just to please my parents. If I agree to marry Jane it would mean I would have to live a troubled life for the rest of my life because my heart belongs to joy and she is the woman I want to marry. As I address this, I humble myself and asked for forgiveness from the Nkuna family for the shame I put them through. Joy, I am sorry for failing you and our son and I refuse to live my life without you from this point forward." I went straight to where Joy was seated, nailed down and ask her to marry me. without any hesitations she said yes and I immediately took out the diamond ring that I had kept on my pocket throughout the event. People couldn't stop celebrating as I was sliding the ring through Joy's finger.

Mother stood up, took out the microphone from me and asked the music band to play something. As music was playing in everyone dancing mother asked me to step outside to have a quick meeting with pastor Mabaso and Joy. we respected her wishes and went into the office to have a meeting just as she requested. On The meeting she gave me an ultimatum. I had to choose between joy and my parents. The ultimatum she was giving me forced my heart to travel back to the day I

denied Joy pregnancy. I did it once and I was not willing to do it the second time. The mansion Joy disappeared on me was the most miserable time of my life that I never wanted to ever experience.

They say true love only come once and if you let go of it you might never find it again. This time I had to give my heart exactly what it wanted as I chose Joy and our son Miracle. My decision had serious consequences which included being disowned by my own parents. Them disowning me did not break me instead it encouraged me to work harder so that I may be able to provide for my own family.

I didn't hesitate taking Miracle with me and moved abroad with Joy. I managed to get a job it's Cuba is a lecturer and played my role as the head of our family. Joy finished a degree in medicine as well and got a job as a doctor at a local hospital. After trying numerous times reaching out to my mother without any luck I decided to let go and let God.

Few years later pastor Mabaso reached out to me and asked for my forgiveness. we managed to mend our father and son relationship before he passed away. For his funeral service I took my small family home to attend and honour him. I still tried my level best to reconnect with mother but she showed no interest at all. As soon as the funeral was done, I took my family back to Cuba and we continued living our lives. Mother remarried and adopted the children her new husband came with. She cut me off completely as if I never existed but that did not surprise me at all because I knew she was capable of such. That troubled me for some time until I accepted that there was nothing I could do to change my predicament.

Today I am a pastor, today I am a pastor of Christ Is Love Ministry in Cuba, where I am also working as a lecturer at Christ is Love Ministry in Cuba. Joy is still saving with pride as a doctor and you say she is a wonderful woman of God as well. Miracle has grown and has two brothers, Marvel and Brave. We are expecting our daughter as we are six months pregnant. Do I regret the choices I made? No, I don't. There was a time when my love story was that of a troubled man until the troubled man inside me got tired of being troubled and decided to live life to the fullest. I chose love, peace, forgiveness and **'joy'**.

www.ingramcontent.com/pod-product-compliance
Lightning Source LLC
LaVergne TN
LVHW012341100826
845148LV00018B/3228